YOU CANNOT SHOOT A POEM

YOU CAN NOT SHOOT A POEM

poems | Paula Closson Buck

LOUISIANA STATE UNIVERSITY PRESS | BATON ROUGE

Published by Louisiana State University Press
Copyright © 2018 by Paula Closson Buck
All rights reserved
Manufactured in the United States of America
LSU Press Paperback Original
First printing

Designer: Barbara Neely Bourgoyne
Typeface: Adobe Caslon Pro
Printer and binder: LSI

Library of Congress Cataloging-in-Publication Data
Names: Buck, Paula Closson, 1957– author.
Title: You cannot shoot a poem : poems / Paula Closson Buck.
Description: Baton Rouge : Louisiana State University Press, [2018]
Identifiers: LCCN 2017056635| ISBN 978-0-8071-6906-3 (pbk. : alk. paper) |
    ISBN 978-0-8071-6907-0 (pdf) | ISBN 978-0-8071-6908-7 (epub)
Classification: LCC PS3552.U3339 A6 2018 | DDC 811/.54—dc23
LC record available at https://lccn.loc.gov/2017056635

CONTENTS

ACKNOWLEDGMENTS

Thanks to the magazines in which these poems first appeared: *Agni:* "Tigers"; *Cadences* (Cyprus): "Dead Zone Vertigo," "The Diplomat," and "The Knight's Apology" (with translations into Greek by Vasso Yannakopoulou); *Connotation Press: An Online Artifact:* "The Negotiation" and "Nostalgia with Boy and Pink Flamingo"; *Crazyhorse:* "Damselfly"; *Gettysburg Review:* "Jesus and the Modern Wonders" and "Landscape with Glowing Rodents"; *Laurel Review:* "Rules of Thumb on Scale"; and *Poetry Northwest:* "The Octopus Prophet."

My deepest appreciation to the Pennsylvania Council on the Arts, the Fulbright Commission, the Ucross Foundation, and Bucknell University for making possible the writing time and the travel that enabled me to start and finish this book.

Thanks to my Cypriot collaborators, Ruzen Atakan and Andros Efstathiou, without whose painterly companionship the poems of "Dead Zone Vertigo" would not have come into being, and to the three translators of those poems, Asliye Dagman, Despina Pirketti, and Vasso Yannakopoulou, who made me look more closely and take ever bigger steps back and forth across the Green Line. Thanks, too, to the poet Lisa Suhair Majaj for her political insights.

I'd be lost without the faithful readers who helped me see more clearly what I'd done and what I hadn't: Jim Buck, Katie Hays, and Shara McCallum.

YOU CANNOT SHOOT A POEM

EASTERN WOMAN'S
LONESOME WESTERN

I ride my pink bicycle
along the highway toward knobby hills.

After a still and cloudless day,
a breeze swells the cottonwoods.

There will be thunder without rain.
My bicycle is not pink

but oxidized red, one speed,
an easy target. The guns

are all invisible from here
and the swollen hallelujahs like wind

as I ride the flat shoulder
of the empty highway

carrying nothing in my basket.
In this pink composure I scare

the night antelope into being.
I look for silhouettes atop the ridge.

Nobody out here and all the guns
are loaded. Poised and erect,

I ride, apace, my bicycle at dusk.
I hear the voice of leaves moving

in the operatic trees.
The hills are distant and bald,

and the pink bicycle, oxidized red
like a sunset, is not really mine but I'm riding it

anyway. Such is my happiness.

I

NIAGARA
EXHIBITION

NIAGARA EXHIBITION

I. JESUS AND THE MODERN WONDERS

The derelict city came in
through the window to my brain,
a sky so dank
the big house grew us like a mold.

And night hung open to the water's falling,
three blocks away, incessant, irreparable.

Jesus moved like a housebreaker in the dark,
picking things up from the bureaus, the buffet,
and putting them back down, taking only what he claimed
was his. My sister and I alone

slept the Jesus dream. We prayed to Jesus
in a family that hoped to God.
And night hung open to our falling.
Downstream, the power station fed

on water siphoned through the upstream intakes,
which now and again sucked in a boat, a fisherman.
Where was Jesus then?

Flying in and out, less like a dove
than a gull fluttering a landing in the cliff
below the geological museum.

He was turning the water to effluent.
But his name was its own electricity.

Believe that the singing of it
was beautiful. Transforming the burdens
of addicts and depressives, the current ran

among the holiest, and also between unlike bodies
that sometimes couldn't resist.

Jesus was the name of so many miseries,

Jesus the miniseries
in which each moment jerked free
of the mishap that was the moment before.

Heaven's by committee and most of my life
is apocryphal, a story that doesn't

make the cut.
Like the freighter *Michigan*, loaded for spectacle
with exotic animals, lurching toward the brink.

It's 1827. A bear who sees what is coming
leaps from the boat into the rapids
of the upper river. Only she
and a one-eyed goose survive.

2. MY FATHER LIKE FATHER HENNEPIN AT THE BRINK

The man in the dark coat hacks ice
three inches deep from mist-crusted snow with an axe.
He is like the first man to record
the Falls in black and white, insomuch that the Universe
does not afford its Parallel.

Like Father Hennepin at the brink,
my father will take in the beauty and the terror.
The waters that do foam and boyl.

It is winter. A few blocks away, his congregation
is dwindling, his wife unhappy.
What will he do when he brings the ice home?
He will leave us then.

When the tourists have gone
to their beds, the wonder-gasp
expired, and daredevils are bundled in their egos
or their graves, when the suicides have
nothing left to die for,
who then will be the water's witness?

3. KID SIGNING WAIVER AT LOVE CANAL

For if a man be placed flat on his back, with his hands and feet
extended, and a pair of compasses centred at his navel, the fingers
and toes of his two hands and feet will touch the circumference
of a circle described therefrom . . .
—LEONARDO DA VINCI

The waiver says he gives up the right
for what's in the tanks he will clean
not to kill him.

Chlorobenzenes trip
the death signal in his cells,
but he is thinking only of the symmetry
connecting him to the universe.
Or the girl who shelves art books at the public library.
The girl as straight as a clean deal.

Since he's finished with Uncle Carmen
and electroshock and LSD,
maybe he's thinking, too, of Jesus. For if a man be placed
flat on his back, with his hands and feet extended . . .

Then it rains so hard
the swimming pools lift out of the ground,
so hard it's almost biblical. Chemical cocktails burble up
at the neighborhood party.

And the kid knows, when that happens, that his body
is not like a universe but a dump.
Described therefrom.
And the moon will have only doomed houses
to shine on while the river works its sorry
dialysis on the neighborhood.

4. THE DRUG DEALER AND THE VIRGIN

If painted by Da Vinci, my sister
would be holding an ermine. But in real life
the dealer gives her a cat. Its name
is Numchuks. The dealer, Lebanese, has a huge black
mustache, even at seventeen, and he is kind
though with the potential for violence.
My sister is a golden girl. Which is to say blonde,
and good as pretty girls go. Though not
like me. I'm a good girl through and through.
Dark and gangly. Harassed at school.

The story of the ermine
is that it would rather die than soil its white fur.
So she does not marry the dealer.
She marries, instead, the boy who loves Da Vinci,
the boy from Love Canal who offers
the promise of salvation.

Everyone said I had a beautiful sister.
We had one cat named Numchuks and one named Lily,
a cat with the potential for happiness.
Everything that comes to pass, read in light of this story.

5. LANDSCAPE WITH GLOWING RODENTS

When my father swept the earth,
it was with a Boy Scout's broom
made of pine boughs. *Leave it cleaner
than you found it* he said.

We had no idea how dirty it was.
How very dirty an earth it was.

In the 1940s, while my studious father pored over
history books at the U of R,
its scientists buried two-hundred-eighty thousand

radioactive mice and rats in the ground near Niagara.
My father plumbed cosmogonies
for Truth but remained untutored

in the two-hundred-eighty thousand glowing rodents,
an eternity in half-lives.

Consider my father who,
like Jesus, was a carpenter. When he said *God,*
he meant birch bark canoes,
meant go where the current takes you.
He meant the love that was failing him.

My father put away his robes, along with the diplomas
in history and divinity.
And the rodents—when finally
someone thought to dig them up—had disappeared.
Leaving not even grave clothes behind.

6. IN BLACK AND WHITE

The girl I was is freezing in a too-short skirt,
her head low, her collar up. School closed
on account of the violence,

she hurries down Pine Avenue toward home.
And the black girls who have taken her coat
shout after her, *Hey, white girl,*
how you even stand on them legs?

Returning to a city gone belly up in radium sludge
and phosgene, a city of race hate and corruption,
of freaks and marvels, of the scams and illusions
that distorted us all,

I think of what it is I want to say. I call
across the derelict frontier,

You should see what I've got for a heart.

7. OIL STUDY FOR A LOST PAINTING

Father Hennepin was known
even by the French as a colossal liar.

And had I merely imagined the happiness
beauty once made possible?

Like the men at factories
powered by the Niagara who at break time
lounged atop sacks of uranium,
eating bologna on Wonder bread.

Then one day Hiroshima. One day Nagasaki.

Or the couples honeymooning at the Radisson
who conceived boys destined to carry
local Agent Orange to Cambodia.

Is beauty just another form of ignorance?

At the failure of an aquarium
three blocks from my old house,
I'm watching blind dolphins veer
into one another in a tiny cement pool.

I pass the defunct Wintergarden and the abandoned
Food King where I once worked.

I want only to see again
the dense water falling into its own perpetual

whirling, frothy and dark below; to witness
the spring-laced trees across the gorge

and not to despair,
when those I loved meant well
but were mistaken, and what I thought was good
was less than true.

II

DEAD ZONE VERTIGO

Varosha, once a world-class tourist resort, has been a ghost city on the divided island of Cyprus since 1974. It was completely abandoned when years of inter-ethnic violence between Greek Cypriots and Turkish Cypriots culminated in a coup inspired by Greece's ruling military junta. Turkey invaded Cyprus and occupied the northern third of the island. Varosha features prominently in negotiations between the Greek and Turkish Cypriots.

WHAT HASN'T BEEN LOOTED IS HARDLY WORTH TAKING

1.

You cannot shoot a poem. And the poet said she had a reservation, not a revolution. No one in the abandoned hotel could find it anyhow.

2.

The elevator is out of service. Even with such heavy bags, ghosts prefer the stairs.

3.

Her reservation is this: Language is not a treaty. Language is not a house.

4.

The elevation of language is pretty—or maybe just petty. Should she lie down in the ruined apartments of the sky and think beauty? (Now that the shelling has stopped.)

5.

Climbing decades skyward, she still believes the glossy brochure with Richard Burton by the sea.

6.

You can shoot a film, but you cannot shoot a poem. You cannot tell the poem where not to look. It's looking at you.

7.

The poet tracks her words across the muddy floor where broken
tiles chatter.

8.

The mattress she lies down on is stained by semen and nocturnal
accident, good blood and bad blood. She's a spy for both sides.

9.

Listen: the voices of gulls and girls from the beach beyond the heavily
guarded chain-link fence.

10.

At first the poet meant beauty, but aren't those soldiers tired?

11.

Their cheeks turned away from the butts of guns, maybe they're
looking at you, awaiting your signal.

DEAD ZONE VERTIGO

The sky moves and you know it
by the clouds.

The tall building moves and you know it
by the sky—

windows all broken, concrete
forgetting

its rigid idea. If you went up you would fall.
Like children or uncles falling

from their vacations where the metal rails of
balconies are torn off.

Remember how we used to lean out
toward the sea?

Mister, you at the negotiating table,
what are you

thinking when the sky moves
and the building

sways and for a moment you are caught
off-balance?

As a person, I mean, just as a man
there looking.

THE NEGOTIATION

I'll take the olive and you keep the lemon.
You have the sea; I'll take the old city.
When we both need bread, we won't ask God,
who long ago abandoned his chair on this beach.

You thought no one lived in the apartments
over the shell-shocked bakery,
but there must be one old refugee

to the highest rooms, who each night lobs
into the sky, like a giant wheel of bread,
the moon of this desecrated planet.

If you've any respect for what we
once were, leave the geraniums.
They don't need either of us.
And I guess I'll take this stray dog here,

since you took bathing in January
in the little bay I loved so well
with the swamped wooden boat.
Though it hardly, now, seems fair.

Why have I given up nearly everything
and you almost nothing at all?

I'll shoot if you try to take the wind.
I want to die under the carob tree.
Leave me that and I will pray for you,

though God has gone from his hiding place
in the highest limbs, and the rats each day
are killing off more of the foliage.

THE KNIGHT'S APOLOGY

When he set out for the Holy Land in 1192, it meant he would defend the destruction he had been about—the raped women and pillaged landscapes. But now, delayed by centuries, his apology means he is, well, sorry. Yes. The knight is sorry for your ancestral hurt. For the dead children. The disemboweled sheep. He's sorry for all of the busted-up mosques and his general insensitivity to the needs of others. He wishes he hadn't spoiled so many beautiful people and places in order to save them. When the knight set out, *to spoil* meant to increase one's possessions. To take what you thought you'd a right to. Now what it means is a dirty shame. When the knight set out, *condominium* meant Christians and Muslims sharing the island. In the vacant space of their violence toward each other, what do these ruined apartments mean? His own corporation gone bust, the knight is riding back through Famagusta. Disarmed, he's stalled in the showroom of this postmodern ruin with the fleet of 1974 Toyotas. He's trafficking in guilt. And he's struck by the fondness he feels for people and real estate that once meant so bloody much trouble. What will you do if you see him there—idling, looking for home? Will you remember your own historic indiscretions? Consider the emptiness of these apartments set at a rakish angle to the sea. Are the shades at the windows returning ghosts, or just what the last person raised or lowered after fleeing or looting the place?

THE PASHA'S SECOND THOUGHTS

Transposed from the eighteenth century, he sits poker-faced behind his mustache at the negotiating table, one hand on the little vial in his pocket. He's ready to poison the coffee if things don't go his way. Each has his forte. Each his fort. Theirs here at Famagusta fell to a few well-sown misconceptions, to braggadocio and the flaying of their Captain Bragodin. But now this weird resort at the seaside looks as gray and gutted as a hacked-up elephant. To see a city abandoned like that somehow takes the pleasure out. And there's no revolt—just an awful, apocalyptic antidote to the impulses that once governed. Was he brash? Did he tax the Christians too hard? Even the Muslims, all holy talk and pride, rose against him, an Ottoman. And he'll be the first to admit he wasn't much good at civil administration. Not even civility, if you put it that way. In the distance, a construction crane frozen in time appears to hover over the shoulder of one of his adversaries across the table, poised to remove the other man to the heaven of lost causes. A heaven they share. No one should end up there. Now someone's coming with a tray of black coffees, but the sea breeze whispers a postmodern courtesy in his eighteenth-century ear, like an unincorporated religion. A wish or a vision. It ruffles his mustache in the weed-filled room.

THE DIPLOMAT

on the resignation of the UN special advisor for Cyprus

The diplomat is a doormat. Only double. When you are coming in, wiping your feet, your enemy is going out, wiping his feet. The diplomat tires of this, understandably. He has visions: weapons into plowshares, sheep and goats living together. You say he'll carve a leg from your animal for himself, but if he hasn't a spit to his name? Not a *souvla*, not a barbecue. If he hasn't a country, a split-level house, a love seat, a toilet, a demijohn to call his own? Where does the diplomat sleep? On a diplomattress. (Not to be confused with the rare female of the species.) He's a joke in the city of your hate. City of an eye for a tooth. Cut off your nose to spite his face. He is not your enemy's friend. He squats in a no-man's-land next to the journalist and the relief team with their bandages and all that spoiling, undistributed food. He's got a diploma in your failure. (*It's almost like cheating!* you cry.) When the diplomat can't sleep, it's your nightmares he's having. He looks out into the courtyard of the hotel after midnight and wonders what he's doing in your country. He can hear the resolutions the weeds are making. They always win in the end. That's his conspiracy theory. Also the truth. In the morning, a shower and another close shave with the intractable. Again, he comes to the table in his down-to-business suit, his flowing robe, his kaffiyeh, his dashiki, his striped tie—fresh, believing that so much is possible. Who can say why?

HANDBOOK ON SUSTAINABLE HATE

1.

Awaken with caution. Open only the right eye.

2.

Keep the blinds halfway down so the tallest trees appear as stumps.

3.

Half the city is the half-truth you can be certain of. Birdsong split at the breastbone is almost something you could hum.

4.

Never drive the back roads on the other side of hate.

5.

Among the lemon trees, you may happen upon the pits your enemies and their children were made to fall into.

6.

Pretend it didn't happen that way. And if your hurt is not yet hate

7.

feed it gristle and bone, feed it histories of hate, hate dashing and medieval. Keep chewing though your teeth be breaking.

8.

The corporations and musclebound nations—they're all behind you now. A testosterone boom or bust dependent on your hate.

9.

Never spit into a napkin, even if your appetite should fail you.

10.

Because your blood is in that soil. And the earth is one huge mass grave anyhow. They can't take that away from

11.

the women in half a country, putting hand-washed hopes on the line to dry,

12.

or the women in the other half, who check the sky and unpin damp sheets quickly

13.

while girls stripped of their passports are falling from the high-up windows of sex clubs. Despite this gentle pleading rain,

14.

trust your heart to men absolute in hate uniforms. Hate suits.

15.

Was there ever a time when we did not hate? (Oh friendship! Oh, boxed-up sweetness in the display case of the soul!) Don't think of that now.

PEACE POEM

The woman does not talk to the man. She is tight-lipped like a border.
She plunges her hands into the dishwater, swiping grease from a can,
rips a clean slit into the opposable part of her thumb.
She mutters the curses of a barbaric anger that feels
centuries old, millennia even, toward the man. She hears the cry
of the people in her chest, moving out in their armor, leaving their barns,
the cows half-milked, surging from the factories, not people but a people,
all she stands for building a barricade against him.

Where are the journalists to record this moment? To hole up in the house
with their laptops and their cameras? Because she is right to hate him.
He said *If you won't I don't know why I should have to,*
he said *Kidney beans would ruin it. We don't have the money.*
I have no idea what Inverness is like. And it was his tone, really—
a condescension she'd previously associated only with the French.
Évidemment. How the French condescended to Africa, to the Caribbean,
even to America when it was sending out its freedom fighters:
that's what he reminds her of, though he isn't French at all,
just a poser with his Sartre and Baudelaire.

At a border they crossed when they were young,
the Greeks inspected the packages only of the Turks, left brown paper
hanging in shreds, twine limp, sweets and personal effects exposed.
And on the way back, the Turks charged entry fees
they claimed were Greek and kept everyone waiting for hours.
Neither Greek nor Turkish, she remembers only how angry she was,
and that she refused to pay.

Now at the border between waking and sleep, she lies
like a mountain range heaved from the earth to prevent
crossings. She'll betray his trust, whisper his secrets to the Persians.

And even when he runs out into the fray in grayed-out underwear,
vulnerable to enemy fire if it might mean ultimate peace, she'll linger
awhile in the trenches, muzzle loaded and trained on
his sorry heart. Only under cover of night will she gather the air-dropped

PSYOP leaflets (*These enemy bon-bons, these matchbooks falling from the sky
are for you, my little cabbage, only for you!*). Only then will she close her eyes
to count the casualties on both sides, like bloodied sheep
that won't jump the fence finally into oblivion—
the dead she'll drag to a wooded area of her dreams.

MEMORY RELEASES ITS PRISONERS
a poem in blank verse

The last time I saw _____
he was scolding the arrogant rooster.
Or there was no rooster. There were no hens.
It was the 14th of _____ and everyone
was waiting for _____. Eager but guarded.

Even then, we must have known what was going on
at the Ministry of _____. I remember

the way the _____ appeared against
billowing clouds, and how you, my neighbor,
looked as though the fault were mine.

Or did I blame myself?
Had I known I would never
_____ so innocently again,
I'd have drowned in my despair.

The trees were loaded with blossoms
and no one should have been dying.

Now we live in _____ and someone else
breaks our chickens' necks.
Or there are no chickens.
There are no guns—
not in our hands now.
We try at the office
to keep our _____ clean.
And spring in the land of our exile

is so lovely

even looking feels like betrayal.

History will _____
our names. But I'd say yours if I thought
I might see you again at _____.

ECO-CITY REBIRTH ELEGY

If bodies in the earth become crocuses
and sheep droppings can make you warm,
if fried potato oil will fuel a car
       (the *taverna* owners were the first to disappear)

and you could pedal a red bicycle
along the green line of loss
       (a sister to soldiers beneath the orange trees)
or along a breakwater built from the rubble of houses

if empty water bottles can become pens become poems,
then what of the power of sadness
       (the had-we-nots, the might-have-beens)
stored in the battery of years
to light the way home?

LOGGERHEADS AT VAROSHA

They hear with tiny, internal ears
the rumor of our extinction.

Unopposed by any light
from these broken-out windows,

they arrive to the blank
expanse of sand

where once we were human.
They'll survive us, settlers here.

Forgive us our trespass on earth
as it is undersea where they

drift above rusted propellers
and the silent beds of fossil fuels.

NOSTALGIA WITH BOY AND PINK FLAMINGO

for G.L.

Toward the extravagance of feathers the boy
is running, across the living room to that wild sweet
      encounter, mouth open in wonder

and time a ballet, costumed in pink, touched
with black at the wings, flying.
      Birdward into the future, he runs

into the shattering, 1973, 1974, he sees sky—
Famagusta blue—sees bird, balcony, blood. His own.
      The glass door stutters its surprise when he

breaks through. Into the fleeing. Boy and bird.
Time, a bullet. Time, the violence that happens every moment
      we can't return. As when barbed wire

becomes the door, and the city is forbidden,
the bird no-love-lost, and we don't see where we're headed
      or what will break us. He has the scars

to prove it. Please. Tell me a story. The one
about the salt marsh by the sea. How lovely the bird,
      how happy the boy running to meet it.

III

BESTIARY

DAMSELFLY

She makes her drollerie

at the margin of the river—

slender stick of a body

in colors costly

to a monk's scriptorium:

scarlet, indigo, viridian.

Prehistoric, diminished

from the size of a hawk,

she's light as stained air—

flies clumsy, her glassy

wings leaded. No angel

she takes one mate

and another, so the male

must gaff and scrape her

of a rival's sperm.

Must lift her, exhausted

from the water when it's over.

Poet with no heart,

she wears her eyes on her sleeve.

Saint with no soul,

she sees in mosaic, passes

millennia. What the sky

wants to tell us

is written in Damselfly,

a language few now living

remember how to read.

TIGERS

In the zoo yard in moonlight
two tigers are sleeping, spine to spine, each mirrored
by the other's lack of intention—the stretch of a forepaw,
the incline of a head. Their synchronous
yawns divide the earth into hemispheres: the great
continents of their backs, the Occident
and the Orient of their rumps. Tails twitch
a memory of differential happiness.

The corridor of their dream is papered in birch.
They sleep without lassitude—
quiet only as cities are quiet, lit and humming
beneath the breath—the repose of yang and yang.

If scholars, they're incestuous, referencing
each other. No master text.
If words, we love them
for having heard them together.
When Blake said *Tyger! Tyger!* he invoked
just one cat—its bold graffiti suggesting a Maker
who had come like a vandal-artist
then slipped back over the wall.
But these two in moonlight

are literalists. When I ask, *What immortal hand or eye?*
or say (of the worn grass) that night has read
the earth's Braille down to nothing,
they lie motionless where the grass is worn—
the great cages of their ribs falling and falling.

ABOUT THESE SHEEP

While some continue munching,
tossing muzzles side to side
in alfalfa, others create channels
of woolen flow,

legless currents in the tide of tall grasses.
Outside Sheridan or Cheyenne,
You come upon these easy sheep
at night.
Shorn, they huddle on warm pavement.
They scare at your approach—

an impulsive cooperative
running that way but then,
all at once, through the field grazed
by the common light or a low-flying cloud,

back again. And would it be unlovely
to stand there eating, comfortable
but alert, awaiting
the ungulate hoof-to-earth that means

in some regions, a kinetic "Shalom,"
in others, more simply, "Shall we?"
and to know that you were getting
the general idea?

Is there any shame
in being shunted with the herd
east-southeast in moonlight?

GUINEA FOWL

Two boy naturalists up early at the compound
in shorts and dark socks wander trepid

in early light, point quiet fingers
at kiskadee and kingbird and devil's guts spilling

from eucalyptus trees. Every leaf
is slant with sound, hoo-hoo

and cock crow, dogs barking
and is it a man shouting

or pigs in the stockyard? Let's say a man
until twenty minutes later when the rank olfactory

assault is launched by hoses
washing intestines from the killing floor,

and the world awakens to the old
notion of inside out. Right side wrong.

Without half trying, the sun lights up
what was the cotton plantation. In the true

spirit of terror, the dictator's sister
who abandoned the place years ago

left behind these guinea fowl
with their tiny, tortured

heads, a spot of blood on each gaunt jowl.
They genuflect to the dirt for ticks,

plump bodies detained
in this world by only the sparest of necks.

THE SEAL IS NOT MY ANGER

She dumps excrement onto the rocks
    and does not cry *Shit!*

She copulates but under duress does not mutter *Fuck!*

Hauled out, she dozes
    with her kind on the sand
at Point Reyes or Land's End.

        Fuck! I cry. *The world*
        is a shitting dump!

But these seals are the fat and satisfied
    slubs of Being.

Not the seven seals
of the Apocalypse—

        though the backs of some are cut
    by the propellers of boats,
            and the males have fought.

While the President makes dirty
    with our dignity,

        taking Christians from his pocket
            to pay eternity,

these seals come clean
    out onto the sand.
            My seven gurus,

they take the long view. They posture and play
 or lie easy by the sea,

plankton-weary. The solitary one lubbing along the beach
 is not the imbecile
 of a cast-off logic.

Two men and a woman stand pointing,
and the hard wind baffles their wonder

that the seals, not dynastic capitalists
 wearing seal-fur coats,

 are Tolstoy-in-winter communal—
in this bad old world, good
 to negative forty degrees.

Shitty old seals,
 hoarse at twilight,
sing me a loafsome song

 so that I can abide
 the ways the world might end.

Because by *world* I mean what's human,
 and all who blubber are not sad.

THE KOI AT URFA

in Ibrahim's pool
these splotchy aberrations
of quiet

what's foiled
is holy what's cosmic a cringe
of movement

beneath corrugated
sky-water these fish and
a mosque moving

targets of reflection
orange alert of the wishful
soul don't be

sore if even
looking disappears
the trees

are in their autumn beauty
and the koi
don't remember lovers

ever sacred and bony
they know only hunger
and oblivion the lily

too sways on its stem
a brain unblooming at dusk
moon on a tether

THE ELEPHANT AND ELLA FITZGERALD

The world is full of simultaneity.
The Brahmin priest, nineteen
and scantily dressed, climbs the back
of a caparisoned elephant

at the same time I enlist
Ella to sing *If you can't sing it,*
you'll have to swing it. At the same time

Ella laments, *Spring can really hang you up*
the most. And I agree. Virtuoso in May,
the elephant bellows down
the articulated octaves
of its need. Its joy. And the priest,

nimble, nubile, is jostled
high above the trainer at the elephant's feet,
who has wielded the chains
of discipline and abuse and now maintains
a calm with leaves and branches.

Exuberant, Ella lets go the bad old life—
the asylum, the reformatory. High Priestess,
she sings ineffable
Moonlight on the Ganges.

Heed that holy scatology,
all the way down to a crazy low
and the little Hindu she hurries in
with a broom at the tail end of ritual.

THE OCTOPUS PROPHET

I saw a small pink octopus on Judgment Day.
It was painted on the chapel wall amid frescoed waves,
the work of an island amateur.

I saw it caught in the teleological crossfire
while bodies stood up from graves
as if from their bathtubs—surprised by strangers—
or when waking after dark from a long and poorly timed sleep.

On land, lions and griffins bore folk in many directions,
valiant in the service of an elaborate system

of blame. The octopus, familiar with the drowned,
hung amid scalloped waves like a cosmic hand towel,
pink and weirded by the artist's hand.

Pressed against the occipital bulb of its head
was the head of a man, the face and some of the hair, and though

a caption in my guidebook said it was disgorging
the head, the octopus seemed rather to be drying it
gently, or bumping it along toward some vague reunion.

While men were dreaming of vindication and women
pleading guilty on all counts, I saw a new Heaven
and a new Earth. And I saw that blithe, pink octopus with eight arms
orchestrating nothing, eight arms of animalian

letting go—the only protagonist in that scenario.
Like the housefly that acts as a kind of prophet in a trompe l'oeil,
persuading us what we're seeing is real.

Though of course, it isn't. We know this especially
if the artist's skill has failed, which in the case of the octopus,
as I said, it had. So I knew there was no afterlife

though all the hatches were flung open,
all the sorry bones unpacked for eternity. And in its mutinous

wisdom, from the stylized deep the octopus chided none of us
in particular when it cried amidst the waste and the glory

Have you lost your head? While the face—

the face just bumped along, furrowed in shame,
swept by a heinous collective dream.

MOTH KOAN

Moths archive the light
    verso and recto

    powdered
they flit and baffle

like a mother-in-law
    on the path to mindfulness

    they toil not neither
do they wear the little wigs

of justice but
    done fretting

    lie down folded

IV
RULES OF THUMB ON SCALE

RULES OF THUMB ON SCALE

There were moments when the world seemed fine ...
—RUPERT BROOKE, ON VENICE

PROXIMITY TO HEAVEN I

The industrial stacks of Mestre
spew smoke
like the intestines of a fish
across the night sky.

STANDING ON THE DOCK

I sway to the wake of a vaporetto just gone.
I will enter civilization

this time through estuaries and vertigo,
the swoon of black water
three feet down the moonlit pilings.

PROXIMITY TO HEAVEN II

The dangling heel of a cherub
who's holding the clouds aloft might graze
the forehead of a man looking up.
(This according to Titian's *Assumption*.)

SIZE IN PROPORTION TO THE VANITY OF HUMAN WISHES

The year Titian died of plague, the unafflicted
piled into boats and steered toward
the island of the lepers, the island of the maniacs,

and the island of the maniacs
of noble or comfortable circumstances but

were turned away.
There was no alone to be
but Titian's great alone.

PROXIMITY TO EARTH

Even the beetles here are made of glass.

AND ONE BOATLOAD OF VEGETABLES

lights up the canal at San Barnaba
long after dark—roseate
greens, artichokes comfortably
Byzantine, potatoes
from planet Earth.

REMEMBER

how your footsteps echoed on stone?
The low, refulgent murmur
of people in cafés around the campo at night?

ONE NIGHT AT A TIME,

we have passed centuries this way,
knitting the days one to another
with our greetings—
always at least one among us

who would live until tomorrow.
Though sometimes
it was wet or cold, and we hurried home

in silence like a scarf knotted at the throat.
Sometimes the city lay under siege.

TODAY: A GARRULOUS SKY

Seven levels of laundry hanging in the street.

IT'S ALL ABOUT SCALE

and everything here, even the divine,
is measured by the proportions of the human body
(exceptions being made)

AS FOLLOWS

Titian's genius
was out of all proportion
to his bitter end, so they violated
the laws of sanitation
and laid him beneath a marble slab
in the church of the Frari.

And when Marco Polo returned
from the Orient with tales to tell,
they called him
Marco of the Million Lies.

Still, they bought his book.
And read about Khan's palace.
And dreamt vermilion silk.

VITREOUS HUMOUR

All night, drunk,
the Adriatic paces outside my door.

All day I see the city as if
through one eye: palazzos in 2-D,
vistas cloud-flattened.

I think of my friend,
an artist who found herself
on the eye ward of the civic hospital,
half blind and speaking
in holiday phrases she'd learned on tape.

Are you comfortable? said the doctor,
an Albanian, in Italian.

You've given the wrong change, she replied.
My pasta is cold. Do you have a room with a view?

BUT NOW, FOR HALF AN HOUR

there is sun on the lagoon,
green water and gray-blue sky

meeting like dignitaries
with brilliant and conflicting ideas
on how peace is to be achieved.

WARS & CAPERS I

Attila the Hun
plundered the Veneto in 452.
Then every hundred years
an invader came along:
the Goths followed by the Lombards,
whom Charlemagne drove off

at the invitation of the locals.
Fifty years later, to found their great cathedral,
Venetian merchants in Alexandria
stole the body of St. Mark.
They carried it out of the harbor
between two quarters of pork.

TWO QUARTERS OF PORK?

Under the noses of the Infidels.

AND DOES THE SPIRIT DWELL IN THE
BONES?

The wind would have run the boat aground
in Romania had the dead saint
not shaken the merchants awake
and told them to take down the sail.

WHO'S TO SAY

Saint Mark wasn't there,
and rattled by the journey?

Or that Santa Clara has not
set up housekeeping
in her own incisor, that villa plucked

from the mouth's lagoon
and displayed at the church of the Frari?

NOSTALGIA BEING WHAT IT IS

one hangs on for dear life.

OR, IN THE WORDS OF ROBERT BROWNING

What of soul was left, I wonder,
when the kissing had to stop?

YOU RETURN TO A CITY AFTER SO MANY YEARS

You return with a mind full of adventures
and begin to unpack, like Marco Polo
back from the Orient, a trunk stuffed
with colorful silks and dirty underthings.

In the morning, you awaken to find the canals
rising like a spidery network of veins
beneath the pale skin at the back of a leg.

Already, again, you're tired of the city—
your own heart pumping effluent
into the lagoon, telling you only the young really matter

in their leather jackets, leather boots,
their voices in the campo at night
like water you won't cross again.

AND IN I FLOUNCED LIKE A CARP

wrote Lord Byron, having slipped
on the marble steps while attempting to mount
his gondola for a rendezvous
with a noble's daughter.

WARS & CAPERS II

But mostly the empire was peaceful.
If you don't count the Crusades,
for instance, and Dandolo who,
blind and geriatric by the Fourth,
would have preferred the comforts of home,
though still, we are told, he *had the cross sewn*
on to his great cotton hat, so determined was he
that all men should see it.

YOU, TOO, MAY BE OLD, BUT NOT TOO OLD

to cakewalk the tombs
in the marble floor of the Frari,
tripping the light fantastic over death,

while Bellini's Saint Benedict
gazes out from the fifteenth-century
doorway of a triptych,
announcing an order
to which you don't belong.

ALTERNATIVE COMFORT IN THE VERY
OLD IDEA OF WATER

There's nothing the color of the Lagoon—
milky, shockingly opaque—
except, perhaps, a scarf of sea-green silk,
no doubt inspired
by the color of the Lagoon.

EVEN CORRUPTED, IT GLITTERS

A cruise ship, cartoonishly big,
slides into the Giudecca Canal behind a tugboat,

palazzos and churches and campaniles shrinking
in its wake, as if to fit the border of a placemat.

Gathered from every nation,
we contemplate the danger

of drowning in our coffee cups,
so small we have become—

SO QUAINT IN MINIATURE, OUR ANNUNCIATIONS

and our torments (*Lady, you know how much?*
as the Nigerians selling handbags say).
The ship obscures everything on the far side,

like a thumb placed between
the eye and the moon.

IT'S OUT THERE TONIGHT

idling at the docks, generators thrumming.
People are sleeping and dancing,
running on treadmills with their earbuds in: people
(don't argue with me here)
in thrall to beauty.

Faster than a dream
can be engineered, the water rises.

A FINAL EXCEPTION TO THE RULE OF THUMB ON SCALE

Near where Titian sleeps in the dark of the Frari,
four giant African caryatids
shoulder a doge's marble tomb.

Their arms bulge with effort. Their heads are bent.
Their great ornery eyes, as big
as moons looking down, say they're skeptical
of the doge's civility.

CODA WITH A SCARF

In the Campo Santa Margherita,
the ex-junkies fold up their table and petitions
and head back to the shelter for the current junkies.
The Nigerians, too, stuff handbags
into a duffel and move in bands
back out to the somewhere they all must sleep,

somewhere in the conglomerate dark,
maybe Mestre. Out and away,
they are moving, maybe closer to heaven,
like the women with henna-dyed hair
who climb the stairs to flats
grown almost too precious to live in.
The Japanese and Brits are drinking late
at Harry's Bar or the Hotel Danieli,

and the players in the band from Peru—
they, too, will leave before long.
But where is the scarf?

THAT SCARF THE COLOR OF THE LAGOON

It may be knotted in the dark
of a locked boutique.
Or you, having jumped from the dock
to this boat already departing, are

WAVING IT

as if to scrawl
your signature on the great
petition of the sky.
You want what you are forever
having to let go. Goodbye, dear Byron,
dear Titian and Henry James.

Peggy Guggenheim and Marco Polo
and Lady Enid Layer, whoever you were;
Vasari, Veronese, goodbye.
So long to the Council of Three
and the Council of Ten. Buono
of Malamocco, Süleyman the Magnificent

(who tried but never made it here),
Demetrius, Despot of the Morea.
Fare thee well, courtesans and junkies
and others unnamed, including

the man who keeps the generator humming
in an open room along the passageway
between Santa Margherita

and San Barnaba, so the night
won't shut down when we sleep.
Even he must go.

THERE NEVER WAS A CITY

that didn't grow
small in the distance, so small
it had to disappear.